EZINE KALEIDOSCOPE JANUARY 2025

MANIFESTING A NEW REALITY

EZINE KALEIDOSCOPE

Made with ♥ on the Notion Press Platform
www.notionpress.com

Contents

Credits

Volume 1 Issue 4 2025
Founder/Editor: Meetu Sehgal
Associate Editor: Chahat Singh
Cover Design: Tony
Graphic Design: Dilip Kumar
Digital Media Marketing: Raza Kamil
Project and Growth Catalyst: Yash Yadav
Business and Market Strategy: Ashi Sharma
Legal Advisor: Arushi Sharma
Owned by Meetu Sehgal
at S-423, Greater Kailash-I, New Delhi – 110048
Published by Notion Press
Contact Information
M: +91 9953753637
E: info@ezinekaleidoscope.com
W: www.EzineKaleidoscope.com

From The Editor's Desk

Dear Reader,

Let me begin by wishing you a very Happy New Year 2025. This is the beginning of the 15th year of the Ezine Kaleidoscope website and this month is our 4th edition in print of this magazine.

Since the New Year begins for many people with resolutions, which unfortunately fizzle out for most by the 3rd week of January, we decided to help you in this area by bringing this edition on the theme of Manifestations.

Resolutions are nothing but trying to deliberately manifest a new reality. They often don't work because we resolve from a conscious mind, thinking and hoping that this time, this year, we will be able to achieve our dreams.

But alas, our subconscious mind has other plans for us. This is part of the mind that is in charge 97 per cent of the time. Its job is to ensure that the programs and beliefs stored here are always implemented and manifested. And we never involved it in this decision-making process. If we are trying to manifest something that does not match or is the complete opposite of the programs, then the manifestation won't happen.

In order to involve the subconscious mind in the manifestation process, we use various techniques like visualizations, practice, repetition, affirmations, emotional healing, inner work etc. We actively work with the energy of the Solar Plexus Chakra and bring our desires into this three-dimensional physical reality.

There are a few things that you always want to remember when it comes to the deliberate manifestation of a new reality –

- **Like attracts like** – so bring your energies in alignment with what you want. Remember abundance attracts abundance. Lack can never receive prosperity.
- **Limiting beliefs are the blocks** – if you believe that miracles can't happen, or that you don't deserve, or perhaps that it's never going to be easy, then these beliefs will always remain true. So, clear them, release them, change them. Use EFT, NLP or any other kind of inner work for this.
- **Being specific** – Universe is an open buffet that is always offering you

what you want. But you need to be very specific about it. It's like ordering food in a restaurant but not being specific about what dish you want. The server will be confused, may get you the wrong order and will most likely take time.

In this edition, you will find many practical guides to manifesting love, health, and relationships as well as a step-by-step guide to making the Law of Attraction work for you. We would love to know what you think about the articles here. Do share your feedback on social media or through an email on info@EzineKaleidoscope.com.

Wishing you a very Happy New Year 2025
Light and Grace

Meetu Sehgal
Founder/Editor Ezine Kaleidoscope
Trainer, Therapist, Healer and Tarot Reader

I

Law of Attraction: A Step-by-Step Guide to Unlocking Your Manifestation Potential

LAW OF ATTRACTION:
A Step by Step Guide to Unlocking
Your Manifestation Potential

The law of Attraction is one of the 12 laws of the universe. The other laws are the Law of Reflection, the Law of Cause and Effect, the Law of Inspired Action etc.

The Law of Attraction states that what you desire will become your reality. At least, this is what the world believes it to be. For a vibrational thought to become a three-dimensional physical reality requires a lot of intense and focused energy. Therefore, practices such as affirmations, vision boards, and visualisations evolved as a part of this practice.

As much as this topic has enchanted people, it has also been a source of vexation and disappointment when despite doing all this, the seeker got minimal to no results. If you are someone who has ever said that the law of attraction works on a fluke or that it's not consistent, then this article is for you.

Let us first understand the premise behind the Law of Attraction to use for manifestation.

Like Attracts Like

The meaning of this phrase is that similar vibrations attract each other, and similar energies will come together.

The law of Attraction states that "like attracts like". The principle of "like attracts like" is rooted in the understanding that everything in the universe, at its core, is energy. Whether it's a physical object, an emotion, or a thought, everything vibrates at a specific frequency. Similar frequencies naturally resonate with each other and are drawn together. This is why negative patterns tend to perpetuate when left unchecked.

When we say "similar vibrations attract each other," we mean that your internal state—composed of your thoughts, feelings, and beliefs—shapes your external reality. For example:

- If you constantly think about abundance and feel grateful, you emit high-frequency vibrations that align with opportunities for abundance.
- On the other hand, if you focus on fear or lack, your lower-frequency vibrations attract situations that reinforce those feelings.

This concept is why people often say, "Money creates more money." It's not the money itself, but the energy and mindset behind it—confidence, sense of abundance, and proactivity—that bring more wealth.

So how come thoughts and desires became a part of this Law?

The Law of Attraction doesn't explicitly state that "what you think will come true." Instead, it emphasizes that what you *consistently vibrate* at the emotional and energetic level becomes your reality. Here's how thoughts and desires fit into this framework:

1. **Thoughts are Vibrational Signals**

    - Your thoughts are among the most refined forms of energy. While physical objects are dense and slower to move, thoughts are light and are instantly broadcast into the universe.
    - When you think a thought, it carries a vibration that interacts with the universe. Repeatedly thinking about something enhances this vibration, signalling to the universe what you are "tuning into."

2. **Desires Focus Energy**

    - Desires act as a magnet for energy by directing your focus and emotions. When you desire something deeply, your emotions—whether excitement, hope, or longing—add power to your thought vibrations.
    - These emotions fuel the manifestation process by aligning your energy with the frequency of what you want.

3. **The Link Between Mind and Body**

    - The physical body is the densest form of vibration and serves as the final stage where manifestations appear. Your thoughts begin the process by creating a blueprint of your desires.
    - Over time, through sustained focus and emotional alignment, this blueprint materializes into physical reality.

Why Like Attracts Like and Not Just Thinking Matters

Merely thinking about something isn't enough to manifest it because your vibrational energy is made of:

- **Your Thoughts**: What you consciously focus on.
- **Your Emotions**: How you feel about those thoughts.
- **Your Beliefs**: The subconscious programs that shape your perception of reality and experiences.

For example, if you think about wealth but feel deep fear about money or hold subconscious beliefs like "I don't deserve to be rich," your vibration becomes inconsistent. This mismatch creates resistance and prevents the manifestation.

Subconscious mind – The Powerhouse

Your subconscious mind is a powerful entity. It is full of programs that you use every day, from how you walk and brush your teeth to how you speak a language and even interpret situations and events. From birth to around age seven, the subconscious operates predominantly in alpha or lower brainwave states, often referred to as the "hypnotic state."

In this state, the mind is recording everything, every piece of information, every behaviour that it observes. This is also known as the learning state. After the age of 7, the brain shifts into beta wave activity, marking the development of the conscious mind. From this point onward, the subconscious continues to drive much of our behaviour, relying on the programs it internalised during those formative years.

How the Subconscious Learns

While the subconscious absorbs information effortlessly in early childhood, learning in later years requires repetition or strong emotional experiences. For example:

- **Repetition:** Practicing a skill, habit, or belief consistently embeds it into the subconscious.

- **Intense Emotions:** Events associated with extreme joy or trauma leave lasting imprints, making the subconscious particularly sensitive to emotionally charged experiences.

We are always manifesting

Our subconscious is constantly perceiving the environment and bringing to our attention opportunities aligned with what it "knows" to be true. Here's the key: the subconscious works to manifest what is familiar—what we are used to experiencing.

This is why our current reality, including our relationships, finances, health, and overall life circumstances, is a reflection of the beliefs and programs stored in our subconscious. These deeply ingrained programs, often referred to as *beliefs,* shape how we perceive and interact with the world. In essence, the subconscious mind creates your reality based on what it believes to be true.

Manifesting something new

If you want to manifest something that is not a part of your experience, for example, financial abundance, a loving relationship, good health, or an easier life—you must first make it a part of your subconscious programming.

The subconscious operates from its familiar programs, so trying to manifest something entirely new without addressing underlying beliefs can lead to frustration. This is why many people struggle with the Law of Attraction; their subconscious programs are not aligned with their conscious desires.

How to Make the Law of Attraction Work for You

1. **Clear Limiting Beliefs**
   Your beliefs are the foundation of your reality. They are your truths according to which you live your life and attract experiences. If your subconscious mind holds limiting beliefs like "I don't deserve wealth", "Healthy relationships are hard to find" or "It can't be this easy," these will

block your manifestations. Start by identifying these beliefs through self-reflection or journaling and shifting them to more empowering ones. Use tools like **affirmations**, **EFT (Emotional Freedom Technique)**, or **guided meditations** to release and replace these beliefs with empowering ones.

2. **Align with Your Desire**
   Manifestation isn't just about thinking; your feelings and emotions play a huge role in it. Align your emotions and energy with the reality you wish to create. For example, if you want to manifest wealth, you cannot do it from a place of feeling scarcity. The vibrations won't match. Remember, like attracts like. Feel abundant and grateful now, even before it shows up in your life. Visualization exercises can help you enter this state by vividly imagining yourself living your desired reality.
3. **Set Clear Intentions**
   The universe responds to clarity. Think of this like going to a restaurant and asking the waiter to bring food without specifying exactly which dish you want to eat. Be specific about what you want. Instead of saying, "I want more money," specify, "I am manifesting $10,000 to pay for my education." Write your intentions down and revisit them daily to keep your focus sharp. Your intentions shouldn't be such that you need to see your diary to say them or remember them. Keep them simple and focused.
4. **Take Inspired Action**
   your intentions and affirmations will begin to draw in the experiences necessary for you to achieve your desires, but you also will need to be ready to make the most of them. The universe also requires your participation. Take steps that align with your goals. If you're manifesting a new job, update your resume, network, and apply for positions. Your actions will signal to the universe that you are serious about your desire.
5. **Cultivate Gratitude**
   Gratitude is a high-vibration emotion that attracts more of what you appreciate. Gratitude gives the signal to the universe that whatever you are manifesting, that vibration is already present and hence more of it can start coming to you. Practice daily gratitude by listing things you are thankful for. This not only raises your vibration but also shifts your focus from lack to abundance.
6. **Detach from the Outcome**
   Detachment doesn't mean you stop wanting what you desire. It means releasing desperation and trusting that the universe is working on your

behalf. Obsessing over your manifestation can lower your vibration and create resistance. Manifestation requires you to **know** that what you want is coming to you. Trust the process and let go of the "how" and "when." Trust the Divine timing. If it doesn't happen in your time, know that it is happening in the divine time which is always for your highest good.

7. **Maintain High Vibrations**
   Manifestation requires a sustained high vibrational state. Incorporate practices like meditation, spending time in nature, and engaging in activities that bring you joy. Avoid negative influences and surround yourself with positivity. Stay away from people who are naysayers or have a pessimistic attitude towards your desires. If there is someone who says something like "This is not possible", in your mind cancel these words by saying "CLEAR, CANCEL, DELETE" to ensure that their attitude doesn't become your attitude.
8. **Work Through Emotional Blocks**
   Emotional blocks, such as fear, doubt, or past trauma, can hinder your manifestation process. Emotional blocks can act like two horses pulling the carriage in opposite directions and no movement happens. Techniques like EFT **(Emotional Freedom Techniques, inner child work**, **NLP (Neuro-Linguistic Programming)**, or therapy can help you address and heal these blocks, creating space for your desires to flow into your life.
9. **Be Open to Receiving**
   Sometimes, manifestations come in unexpected forms. This requires you to widen your gaze and relax instead of hyper focussing on the end result. Stay open to opportunities and signs from the universe. Trust that what you receive will align with your highest good, even if it looks different from what you imagined.
10. **Practice Patience**
    Manifestation is a process, not an instant result. Keep your focus and faith strong while allowing the universe the time it needs to orchestrate the best possible outcome.

Manifestation is not just about what you want but about who you are becoming in the process. By aligning your thoughts, emotions, and actions with your desires, you create a harmonious flow that allows the universe to bring your dreams into reality.

Start with manifesting little things of no consequence to you to build your muscle of trust in the universe. Then move on to deliberately manifesting things that matter. This process requires you to not trust, but know that it will happen because this is nature, this is the Law of the Universe. It's already happening every day. You are just trying to do it deliberately now.

About the Writer

Meetu Sehgal

Meetu Sehgal is a Personal Transformation and Emotional Wellness Coach, EFT Trainer, Tarot Reader, Author, Reiki Grandmaster and Counselling Psychologist. With more than 15 years of experience in her field, she has been passionately working with individuals, helping them resolve health, wealth and relationship challenges through coaching. Meetu Sehgal is an MBA graduate from Delhi University and also holds a Masters in Psychology. Passionate about writing and spirituality, she has blended both in her work, which has helped hundreds of people around the world find peace within themselves. Her latest book, "Happy Inside Out", is a definitive guide to understanding and handling emotions and moods.

II

Manifesting Love: Building Healthy Connections Through Self-Belief

MANIFESTING LOVE
Building Healthy Connections
Through Self-Belief

Love is one of the most profound experiences we can manifest into our lives. It holds the power to heal, transform, and elevate our existence. However, the journey toward manifesting love and a healthy relationship often begins with an inner exploration of our beliefs, trust in the universe, and the courage to let go of what no longer serves us.

The Role of Limiting Beliefs in Love

At the heart of manifesting a loving and healthy relationship is understanding our limiting beliefs. These are the subconscious thoughts and narratives we carry about ourselves, love, and relationships. Often rooted in past experiences, childhood conditioning, or societal norms, these beliefs can create barriers that prevent us from truly receiving the love we desire.

For instance, if you grew up witnessing dysfunctional relationships, you might internalize the belief that love is painful or fleeting. Similarly, a history of rejection can lead to a fear of vulnerability, making it difficult to open your heart fully. These beliefs become self-fulfilling prophecies, as we attract relationships that mirror our inner doubts.

Recognizing these limiting beliefs is the first step toward breaking free from them. Engage in practices like journaling to explore your subconscious patterns, seek guidance from a therapist or coach, or practice affirmations that rewrite your inner narrative. For example, affirmations like "I am worthy of love," and "I attract relationships that support my highest good" can help shift your mindset and energy.

Bringing Clarity to Your Love Life

Sometimes, the biggest obstacle to manifesting love is a lack of clarity about what we truly desire in a relationship. We may consciously have an idea of what love and a healthy connection look like, but our subconscious beliefs can contradict this vision. To align these aspects, it's important to bring clarity to your love life.

Here are steps to help you gain clarity:

1. **Reflect on Past Relationships:** Take time to assess what worked and what didn't in your previous relationships. Identify patterns, lessons, and red flags that you want to avoid in the future.

2. **Define Your Ideal Relationship:** Write down what you desire in a partner and a relationship. Be specific but flexible. Include qualities, values, and the type of connection you want to cultivate.
3. **Identify Non-Negotiables:** Determine the boundaries and values that are most important to you. This will help you avoid settling for less than you deserve.
4. **Examine Subconscious Beliefs:** Use tools like journaling or guided meditations to uncover any conflicting beliefs about love. For instance, you might consciously want a stable relationship but subconsciously fear intimacy due to past hurts.
5. **Visualize Your Ideal Relationship:** Close your eyes and imagine what it feels like to be in the kind of relationship you desire. Focus on the emotions, energy, and joy it brings, rather than just the physical details.
6. **Align Your Actions with Your Intentions:** Take steps that reflect your readiness for love. This could include working on self-improvement, practicing self-care, or engaging in activities that bring you joy and confidence.

Trusting the Universe and Letting Go

Manifesting love is not solely about setting intentions; it's about surrendering control and placing trust in a higher power. Many of us struggle with the idea of letting go because we fear losing control. Yet, true manifestation requires us to release attachment to how and when our desires will come to fruition.

Placing trust in the universe means believing that it has our best interests at heart. Sometimes, the process of manifesting love may seem chaotic. Relationships or situations that are misaligned with your higher purpose may start to crumble, and life might feel turbulent. This is not a sign of failure; it's a sign that the old is breaking down only to make way for the new.

One of the most profound lessons I learned while practicing manifestation was the importance of letting go. I discovered that clinging to old patterns, people, or expectations kept me stuck in a cycle of scarcity and fear. It was only when I released these attachments and self-sabotage, I was able to clearly envision and make space for love and joy in my connections deeply.

When Manifestations Feel Unfulfilling

Sometimes, when we finally receive what we've been manifesting, we realize it's not as fulfilling as we expected. This can be a moment of deep introspection and growth. It's important to understand that this is not a failure but an opportunity to gain even greater clarity about what truly aligns with your heart and soul.

If you find yourself in this situation, it's crucial to continue letting go of what doesn't feel right and refining your vision of what love means to you. Settling for less than you deserve is another form of self-limiting behaviour that keeps you unhappy and unfulfilled. Manifestation is a dynamic process, and your desires and needs may evolve over time. Honour this evolution and trust that the universe will bring you closer to what resonates with your highest good.

The Power of Detachment

Detachment does not mean giving up on your desires; it means releasing the fear of not achieving them. This subtle yet powerful distinction shifts your energy from desperation to abundance. When you let go of the need to control outcomes, you allow the universe to work its magic.

Practicing detachment involves focusing on your personal growth and joy. By cultivating self-love, pursuing your passions, and nurturing your well-being, you raise your vibrational energy. This magnetic energy naturally attracts the right people and experiences into your life. Trust that the universe knows what is best for you, even if the journey looks different from what you imagined.

Navigating the Transition

As you manifest love and happiness, be prepared for some discomfort. Things that no longer align with your energy will fall away, and this can be unsettling. It may feel like life is falling apart, but in reality, it's falling into place. Trust the process, even when it's messy.

For example, you might experience the end of relationships or situations that no longer serve your highest good. While this can be painful, it's a necessary step in clearing the path for new blessings. Embrace these moments as opportunities for growth and transformation.

Celebrate the small victories along the way. Each step you take to heal your limiting beliefs, practice self-love, and trust the universe is a step closer to manifesting the relationship you desire. Keep a gratitude journal to acknowledge the progress you've made and stay aligned with positive energy.

Remember

Manifesting love and a healthy relationship begins with believing you are worthy of it. By addressing limiting beliefs, gaining clarity on your desires, trusting in a higher power, and letting go of the old, you create space for the new to enter. Remember, the universe always responds to your energy, so align yourself with love, joy, and gratitude.

Letting go is not a loss but a powerful act of faith. Trust the process, surrender your fears, and watch as the most beautiful blessings unfold in your life. With patience, self-love, and trust in divine timing, you can manifest the love and happiness you deserve.

About the Writer

Ashi Sharma

Ashi Sharma is a multi-faceted professional and an inspiring force in the realms of personal development and holistic healing. As an author, expressive arts therapy practitioner, EFT practitioner, tarot healer, and podcaster at Breaking Mythos, she brings a unique blend of insights to her work as a Reiki master, lifestyle and business coach and consultant. She has been honoured in the BW Wellbeing World 30 Under 30 Awards for the year 2022 and 2023. Her latest work is part of a beautiful coffee table book, 'Mythology' enriched with hand-painted illustrations that bring ancient stories and legends to life. In this book, she talks about the spiritual journeys of Shukracharya and Odin.

III

Manifesting a New Reality in the Digital Age

Manifesting a New Reality
in the Digital Age

Rapid technological advancements and artificial intelligence have dominated the multiverse we currently live in, making it easier and more relevant to balance human essence with machine logic. This impacts the younger generation as they grow up amidst digital noise with infinite possibilities. This provides a unique opportunity to harness ancient wisdom with modern tools to manifest a life of purpose, joy, and fulfillment.

Manifestation, once considered a mystical practice, has now found a contemporary context where technology can enhance, not hinder, the spiritual process. Let's explore how to weave these two worlds together, creating a harmonious path to a new reality.

The Heart of Manifestation

Manifestation is the art of consciously shaping your life by aligning your beliefs, emotions, and actions with your goals. It's not just wishful thinking; it's a conscious effort to connect with the universe's creative energy. The ancient Indian scriptures, like the Vedas and Upanishads, reflect this idea, emphasizing the profound connection between thought and reality.

The **Brihadaranyaka Upanishad** says:

"You are what your deep, driving desire is. As your desire is, so is your will. As your will is, so is your deed. As your deed is, so is your destiny."

In this modern era, where technology shapes our external world, our inner world remains ours to cultivate and manifest. Harnessing both dimensions can lead to a life of balance and abundance.

Technology and Manifestation: Partners in Creation

Technology might seem incompatible with spirituality, but it is not inherently a barrier—it's a tool. When used mindfully, AI and tech innovations can amplify our efforts to manifest our dreams. However, they must be employed with intention rather than as distractions.

How Technology Supports Manifestation

1. **Visualization Tools**: Apps like Pinterest and Canva help create digital vision boards, offering constant visual reminders of your goals.
2. **Mindfulness Apps**: Platforms like Calm and Headspace guide users toward focus and inner clarity, essential for effective manifestation.
3. **AI-Driven Learning**: Personalized AI tools recommend resources like books, podcasts, and courses, expanding your spiritual and intellectual growth.
4. **Habit Trackers**: Apps like Habitica or Notion keep you consistent in actions aligned with your goals, bridging intention and effort.

Your smartphone can be seen as a modern-day **yantra**—a sacred instrument to focus on your energies. But balance is key: while technology can illuminate your path, your spiritual essence must remain the guiding force.

Steps to Manifestation in the Digital Era

1. **Clarity of Intention:** The first step to manifest is knowing what you want. Vague wishes lead to indefinite results. Reflect deeply on your goals and align them with your values. Write them down in specific terms:

    - Instead of saying, "I want success," clarify: "I want a career that lets me help others while growing financially."

2. **Affirmations:** Use affirmations to align your subconscious mind with your desires:

    - *"I am capable of achieving my dreams with ease and joy."*
    - *"Opportunities flow to me effortlessly."*

3. **Visualization:** Picture yourself living the reality you desire. Apps and tools can help, but the real magic lies in your emotions. Feel the joy of your goals as if they've already become a reality.
4. **Take Inspired Action:** Manifestation requires action. If you dream of becoming an artist, start creating regularly, even if it's a small step.
   As the **Rig Veda** reminds us:
   "Man gains wealth by self-effort, and destiny guides those efforts."

5. **Practice Patience and Trust:** Trust the process. Believe that the universe's timing is perfect, even when results take longer than expected.
   The **Bhagavad Gita** teaches us:
   "You have the right to perform your duty, but not to the fruits of your actions." (Nishkama karma)

Navigating Challenges in a Digitally Distracted World

The younger generation often grapples with impatience and self-doubt, amplified by social media's curated realities. These struggles can obstruct the manifestation process.

Overcoming these requires conscious efforts:

- **Digital Detox**: Step away from screens to reconnect with your inner self.
- **Practice Gratitude**: Focus on what you already have. Gratitude raises your vibration and attracts more abundance.
- **Supportive Communities**: Surround yourself with people who inspire and uplift you.

Ancient Wisdom for Modern Souls

The Vedas and Upanishads consistently remind us of the interconnectedness of life and energy. The mantra ***"Tat Tvam Asi"***—*"You are That"*—teaches us that we are not separate from the universe but co-creators of our reality.

A Simple Manifestation Ritual:

1. **Morning Reflection**: Sit in silence, visualize your goals, and feel gratitude for them as if they've already happened.
2. **Mantra Chanting**: Recite ***"Om Shreem Namah"*** to invoke abundance.
3. **Evening Gratitude**: Reflect on small wins from the day and thank the universe for progress.

The Role of Patience and Trust

This world is filled with instant gratification, and patience feels alien, yet it is the cornerstone of manifestation. Like planting a seed, your dreams need time to grow. Trust that the universe is working behind the scenes, aligning circumstances for your highest good.

Why Trust Matters

1. **It Builds Resilience**: Believing in the process helps you stay committed, even during delays.
2. **It Opens Doors**: Trusting the universe allows you to recognize opportunities you might otherwise overlook.

Remember, even AI—despite its current sophistication—required years of unseen effort to become what it is today. Your manifestations will bloom with the same patience and care.

Practical Manifestations for the Digital Generation

Here are some simple manifestations aligned with modern life:

1. **Manifesting Confidence**:
    - Affirmation: *"I am worthy and capable."*
    - Action: Start small—speak up in meetings or share your ideas online.
2. **Manifesting Fulfilling Relationships**:
    - Affirmation: *"I attract loving and supportive people into my life."*
    - Action: Join communities or attend events aligned with your interests.
3. **Manifesting Financial Abundance**:

- Affirmation: *"Money flows to me effortlessly as I create value."*
- Action: Explore side hustles or invest your time in learning financial management.

Manifesting Together: The Power of Collective Intentions

Collective manifestation amplifies individual efforts. Whether it's a group meditating for peace or a global movement advocating for change, shared energy creates ripples that transform the world.

Platforms like Change.org or GoFundMe exemplify how technology can unite collective intentions to manifest large-scale change.

As the **Atharva Veda** says:

"Let your thoughts be one; let your hearts be one; let your resolve be one, so that you may work together in harmony."

Co-Creating with the Universe in the Digital Age

Manifesting in the age of AI and technology isn't about choosing between ancient wisdom and modern tools; it's about harmonizing the two. By aligning your inner intentions with your external actions and using technology mindfully, you can create a life that is both spiritually fulfilling and materially abundant.

As **Swami Vivekananda** said:

"Arise, awake, and stop not till the goal is reached."

The future isn't just about AI algorithms; it's about the conscious creators who shape the world with intention, patience, and trust. Let that creator be you.

A Manifestation Mantra for Today's World

> "*"I embrace the power of my thoughts, the wisdom of the ancients, and the tools of technology to create a life of purpose, joy, and abundance. I trust the process, and I am grateful for every step on this journey."*"

About the Writer

Chahat Singh

Deeply drawn to spirituality, Chahat is an aspiring content writer with a passion for crafting meaningful narratives. With a bachelor's degree in History and English, she is currently pursuing her masters in English. She finds inspiration in exploring the realms of inner peace and self-discovery, blending pursuits with a reflective outlook on life.

IV

Turning Barriers into Bridges: A Manifestation Journey

Turning Barriers into Bridges

Manifestation is about turning thoughts into reality, but to do so, you must overcome the invisible barriers within—your limiting beliefs. My journey to improve my English skills is a testament to how clearing inner doubts can open doors to endless possibilities.

Since childhood, I've mostly spoken my native language, making it the one I'm most familiar with.

I completed my SSC at a Gujarati-medium school, and even during my graduation from Mumbai University, English wasn't a part of my daily life. Although I taught students during that time, the use of English remained minimal, leaving me with a lack of confidence in the language.

Later, as a junior accountant, I rarely needed English in my professional environment, which further limited my exposure to it. Over time, I became unfamiliar with the root meanings of many commonly used English words. This lack of familiarity made me doubt my ability to form proper sentences, and my self-confidence dwindled.

These limiting beliefs deeply affected me when I entered the business world. I found myself second-guessing my sentences and hesitating to work with clients, especially one-on-one or with global clients. I realized that I had never actively worked on improving my English skills and that it was time to step out of my comfort zone.

One day, I had a wake-up call. Watching others thrive while I felt stuck made me ask myself: *Why am I sitting on the sidelines while others are moving forward?* This discomfort pushed me to reflect on my life goals.

I've always wanted to leave a legacy—to be remembered for something impactful. Writing books has been one of my dreams, but I knew this dream required a strong grasp of the English language. That realization was a turning point.

When I feel uncertain about my next steps, I take a moment to talk to myself. Through positive self-talk, I remind myself that challenges are opportunities in disguise. This habit of self-reflection has helped me tackle external challenges with a stronger mindset.

Improving my English skills has not only enhanced my professional life but also brought significant personal growth. I'm now more confident in expressing myself and navigating conversations. This journey is closely tied to my dream of becoming a published author someday. I've promised myself to master the English language as a crucial step toward building a better future.

How I Started Overcoming Limiting Beliefs

This year, I took intentional steps to address my doubts about English:

1. **Daily Writing Practice**: I wrote something every day, even if it was just a small paragraph.
2. **Learning Through Mistakes**: While working with clients, I made errors but treated them as opportunities to improve.
3. **Seeking Feedback**: I asked for constructive criticism on my written and spoken English.

One of the most powerful lessons I've learned is that action is the antidote to self-doubt. By working with clients, I confronted my fears head-on. Yes, I made mistakes, but each one taught me something new.

Tackling New Challenges

Even as I made progress, doubts continued to creep in. For instance, I often wondered: *How can I write content for my clients' businesses when I'm still working on my own skills?*

This made me realize that limiting beliefs never fully disappear—they evolve. What matters is how you respond to them. To tackle this, I focused on developing consistent habits. I began writing articles regularly and sharing my thoughts online.

Through these efforts, I noticed small wins. Clients started appreciating my work, and my confidence grew. I learned that progress isn't about perfection—it's about persistence.

Lessons from Overcoming Limiting Beliefs

Overcoming limiting beliefs is a process, not a one-time event. Here are some key lessons I've learned:

- **Beliefs Can Change**: We aren't born with a fixed mindset. Our beliefs develop over time and can be reshaped with effort and awareness.
- **Action Builds Confidence**: The more you take action, the weaker your limiting beliefs become. It's like building a muscle—you get stronger with practice.

- **Mistakes Are Part of Growth**: Every mistake is a step forward if you choose to learn from it.

Practical Tips for Readers

If you're struggling with self-doubt or limiting beliefs, ask yourself these questions:

1. What's holding you back?
2. What specific area do you want to improve?
3. What small actions can you take today to move forward?

Here's what worked for me:

- **Start Small**: Don't overwhelm yourself. Begin with manageable steps, like writing a few sentences daily or practicing simple conversations.
- **Use Tools and Resources**: I used apps, online courses, and grammar tools to enhance my skills. Find resources that suit your needs.
- **Be Patient with Yourself**: Progress takes time. Celebrate small wins along the way.

As I continued my journey, I noticed a ripple effect. Improving my English not only boosted my confidence but also unlocked new writing opportunities.

This experience also taught me the value of vulnerability. Sharing my struggles with language and self-doubt resonated with people. It showed them they aren't alone and that growth is possible for everyone.

Moving Forward

Today, I feel more empowered than ever. Writing has become a habit, and my fears no longer dictate my actions. But the journey isn't over. I know I'll face new challenges, but I'm ready to tackle them with the same determination.

If you're on a similar path, remember this: overcoming limiting beliefs requires intentional effort and belief in your abilities. Don't let doubts hold you back.

Think of limiting beliefs as a virus—a "corny virus" that spreads if left unchecked. The cure is belief in your potential, sprinkled with action and persistence.

Take that first step. Challenge your doubts. Remember, your growth is in your hands.

About the Writer

Ruchita Waghela

I am a social media content creator with three years of experience and a writer for over a year. Passionate about creating value through writing, I have authored 64 articles on Medium, focusing on health, self-improvement, mindfulness, and LinkedIn strategies.

I spent 1.5 years discovering my niche and building the discipline habits to write mindfully. Currently, I help B2B agencies, wellness brands, and VCs grow their presence on LinkedIn.

V

Manifestation Through the Divine Feminine: Goddess Laxmi, Isis, and Brigid

MANIFESTATION THROUGH THE DIVINE FEMININE:

Goddess Laxmi, Isis, and Brigid

Manifestation, the act of turning dreams into reality, has been a central theme in mythology, often represented by powerful goddesses whose stories inspire us to harness their energies. Goddess Laxmi, Isis, and Brigid are three such figures who embody the principles of abundance, transformation, and creativity, guiding us on the path to manifesting our deepest desires.

Goddess Laxmi: The Harbinger of Prosperity

In Hindu mythology, Goddess Laxmi is revered as the goddess of wealth, prosperity, and good fortune. Her very presence signifies abundance in all forms—material, spiritual, and emotional. Legends tell of her emergence from the churning ocean of milk (Samudra Manthan), a symbol of her ability to bring forth treasures from the depths of chaos. Laxmi's energy encourages us to align our intentions with hard work and devotion, fostering an environment where prosperity naturally flows. By invoking her blessings through prayers or meditative visualization, we can attract opportunities and resources to manifest our dreams.

Isis: The Alchemist of Transformation

The ancient Egyptian goddess Isis is a powerful symbol of magic, wisdom, and resilience. Her story is one of manifestation through determination and divine alchemy. When her husband Osiris was dismembered by his brother Set, Isis used her magical abilities to piece him together and restore life, showcasing her unparalleled power to manifest transformation against all odds. Her energy teaches us to trust our inner power and intuition, reminding us that with focus and intent, we can rebuild and transform any aspect of our lives. Rituals inspired by Isis often involve affirmations, sacred symbols, and the invocation of her guidance to manifest healing and renewal.

Brigid: The Creative Manifestor

Brigid, the Celtic goddess of poetry, healing, and smithcraft, represents the manifestation of creative energy. Her domain spans the forge, where raw materials are transformed into tools, and the hearth, where ideas become nourishing realities. Brigid's stories often center on her ability to bring light and inspiration to those in need, as seen in her association with Imbolc, a festival of renewal and hope. Her energy inspires us to channel creativity and passion into tangible outcomes, reminding us that manifestation often begins with a spark of inspiration and grows through focused effort and craftsmanship.

Harnessing Their Energies for Manifestation

To channel the energies of these goddesses for manifestation:

1. **Goddess Laxmi**: Create a sacred space with her image, light a diya (lamp), and chant mantras like "Om Shreem Mahalakshmiyei Namah" to attract abundance and remove obstacles.
2. **Isis**: Meditate with symbols like the ankh or wings, focusing on transformation and resilience. Visualize your goals taking shape through her divine alchemy.
3. **Brigid**: Light a candle and write your intentions as poetry or affirmations. Embrace creativity to transform your ideas into actionable steps.

By connecting with the divine feminine energies of Laxmi, Isis, and Brigid, we can align our intentions with universal forces of abundance, resilience, and creativity. Their timeless stories remind us that manifestation is not just about wishing for change but actively creating it with trust, focus, and unwavering belief in our power to transform dreams into reality.

About the Writer

Ashi Sharma

Ashi Sharma is a multi-faceted professional and an inspiring force in the realms of personal development and holistic healing. As an author, expressive arts therapy practitioner, EFT practitioner, tarot healer, and podcaster at Breaking Mythos, she brings a unique blend of insights to her work as a Reiki master, lifestyle and business coach and consultant. She has been honoured in the BW Wellbeing World 30 Under 30 Awards for the year 2022 and 2023. Her latest work is part of a beautiful coffee table book, 'Mythology' enriched with hand-painted illustrations that bring ancient stories and legends to life. In this book, she talks about the spiritual journeys of Shukracharya and Odin.

VI

Solar Plexus Chakra: Inner Fire of Manifestation

THE SOLAR PLEXUS CHAKRA
AND MANIFESTATION

When we talk about gut feelings, we think it's the voice of our heart, but actually, it's not the heart but our solar plexus. You can feel in your belly when something is exciting, the "butterfly" feeling. You can also feel it on your belly when you are nervous or lacking confidence.

The Solar Plexus, also called the Manipur chakra, is very important and is relevant to whether you stand in your own power and continue to achieve all that you must achieve in your present incarnation. Most people are interested in how to open their third eye chakra or activate their crown Chakra, but they don't realise that the Solar plexus is vital.

The word "*Manipura*" comes from "*mani*", meaning "gem", and "*pura*", meaning city. So quite literally, this energy centre is known as the city of gems. In Ayurveda, it is known as Agni. Thus, the element of the Manipur chakra is fire. The Solar Plexus Chakra is located above the belly button. The colour associated with the Manipur chakra is yellow. The organs associated with the Solar Plexus chakra are the central nervous system, skin, digestive organs, liver, and pancreas.

Manipur, or Solar plexus chakra, is not only the intuitive centre but also the centre of power and manifestation. Our personal power, personality, self-esteem, sense of worth and sense of shame are associated with the Solar Plexus Chakra.

The Manipur chakra is deeply connected with our digestion, specifically digestive fire, also called "*Jathar agni*". I'm specifying digestive fire because not only does that fire help you move food along, but it also helps you process the thoughts, feelings, and sensory impressions you get from your surroundings and people around you.

Not enough people pay enough attention to this particular energy centre. Our mental and physical health is related to the Manipur chakra. The Manipur chakra allows you to decide that you will achieve a particular thing and gives you the drive that you require to make it through every obstacle in the process. It is literally the fire lit inside you to drive you to accomplish great things.

According to Vedas, the Manipur chakra reigns supreme from the age of 15 to 21 years old. At this time, you will start to reveal who you are as an individual, in terms of your goals and dreams, what you intend to accomplish, how disciplined you are and much more.

This chakra is responsible for making you feel like you "ought to do something" with your life, still, not everyone has a clue what that "something" is! So, the usual story is that people begin to try all sorts of things, and as a result, they suffer a lot. So, clarity is a must in what you want to manifest.

Your Solar Plexus Chakra is where your personal power lies. If your confidence and self-esteem are low, then you need to work on your Manipur chakra. This energy centre controls the level of freedom you feel. If you feel you are bound by societal constraints, someone else's expectations, or even your unreasonably high expectations, then your chakra is not balanced.

This energy centre helps you establish your autonomy as a unique person. It helps you exercise your will and personal power to accomplish whatever you want to. It's also responsible for your body's metabolism. This centre is connected to your mid back, stomach, gallbladder, liver, adrenal glands, intestines, kidneys, and more.

Benefits of Healing Manipur Chakra

- You will have more empathy and compassion for others.
- You will start attracting opportunities.
- You will experience stability in life.
- You will be enthusiastic and confident.
- You will have better focus and concentration.
- You can enhance the power of manifestation.

Healing your Manipur Chakra

To heal your Manipur, you can use crystals like lemon quartz, yellow Jasper, Citrine, tiger eye, Amber, and sunstone.

The Solar plexus chakra is related to willpower, to achieve your goals. If you activate and heal your Manipur chakra, your manifestation process is faster and more automatic.

Here are a few affirmations to heal your Manipur chakra.

"I am Creative"

"I am boundless"

"I feel free and honour my emotions"

Guided Visualisation Meditation for Manipur Chakra

(You can record in your own voice and play)

- Sit in a comfortable position and close your eyes.
- Notice your breath. If you notice your attention is drifting off, you can bring your mind back to your Solar Plexus.
- Notice that you have a fairly small ball of light that glows yellow.
- As you breathe in, notice how this light grows. As you exhale, notice how you are starting to glow with a yellow light.
- Allow this yellow light to encompass your entire stomach and chest. Feel it as it grows to cover your entire upper and lower body.
- Know that this is the light that drives you. This light is the embodiment of your dreams and aspirations. It is the fire that drives you to fulfil your destiny in life.
- Feel how warm and powerful it is as it moves through your whole body, beginning with your abdomen. Notice how it washes over your throat, head, and lower body.
- Feel this yellow energy infusing you with passion, enthusiasm, and fun. Feel your inner self awakened to the challenge of life, ready to take things head-on with a smile on your face.
- As you breathe out, feel the relief of knowing that you have overcome every obstacle.
- Now, you may begin to chant RAM....RAM..RAM... a couple of times.
- Bring your breath back to a normal state.
- Notice that the yellow light still surrounds you. Pay attention to the way the light pulses powerfully from your solar plexus. With each pulse on your inhale, notice how infused you are with so much passion and joy for life.
- Repeat the following affirmations either out loud or in your mind: “I can feel my personal power, and it is great. I am strongly driven to bring all my dreams to pass. I am on the path to fulfilling my destiny. Everything I touch turns to gold. I am successful in all that I do. I know what it is I want to accomplish, and I remain focused. Ideas come to me easily and quickly. I implement these great ideas with great success. I always see the results of my labour. My word is my bond, and I always do what I say I will. I am always willing to do the most in order to achieve my big dreams. I firmly believe in what I want to achieve. I firmly believe in myself and my abilities. I confidently go after my dreams because they are a done deal.”

- Continue to bask in this pure yellow light and silence as you allow it to energise you, body, mind, and spirit. Inhale this yellow light and allow it to charge your being. Let it fill you up from head to toe, and feel the thrill of it moving around you.
- Bring your attention back to the breath. Whenever you are ready slowly open your eyes.

About the Writer

Prathma

Prathma is an expert in various methods of "Wellbeing and Alternative Healing" Modalities. She has been practising & teaching Reiki & other healing Modalities since 1999. A teacher of love and self-acceptance, she brings light and optimism to anyone who meets her. She believes in a holistic approach with a combination and different healing modalities where intuition and logic, science and spirituality go hand-in-hand. Her simplicity and expertise makes the techniques work like powerful charms that have been helping thousands of people around the globe.

VII

Beyond Resolutions: Recipes for Wholesome Growth

BEYOND RESOLUTIONS:
Recipes for Wholesome Growth

As the New Year unfolds, January is the perfect time to embrace fresh beginnings, set intentions, and work toward manifesting a healthier, more fulfilling life. True growth – be it physical, mental or emotional—starts with a vision backed by intent, a willingness to love our imperfections, and the courage to step beyond the fear of our thoughts. This year, let's break free from health myths and commit to an authentic journey of wholesome well-being.

Setting Intentions for Wholesome Growth

Manifestations begin with intent. When you focus on a vision of health and growth, you set the tone for transformative actions. Wholesome well-being doesn't mean chasing perfection – it's about embracing who you are while striving for balance.

Start by Visualizing Your Goals:

- **Physical Wellbeing**: Envision a strong, nourished body that supports you in daily life.
- **Mental Wellbeing**: Picture a mind clear of negativity, buzzing with creativity and resilience.
- **Emotional Wellbeing**: Imagine a heart open to self-love, forgiveness, and deeper connections.

By cultivating gratitude and speaking kindly to yourself, you align with the reality you wish to manifest.

Overcoming the Fear of Thoughts and Taking the Leap

Fear of failure, judgement, or inadequacy can often prevent us from reaching our goals. Understand that thoughts are not truths; they're temporary visitors. Acknowledge them, but don't let them control your path.

Take action even if it feels uncomfortable. Start small—whether it's trying a new recipe, joining a fitness class, or practising mindfulness. Each small step builds momentum towards your future self.

Loving Your Flaws and Breaking Health Myths

Health is often portrayed as an unattainable ideal—perfect diets, flawless skin, or six-pack abs. These myths can create unrealistic expectations and discourage true self-care.

- **Flaws are beautiful:** Stretch marks, scars, or days when you feel off-track; are all part of your story.
- **Diets aren't one size fits all:** Focus on sustainable habits rather than extreme measures.
- **Rest is Productive:** Your body needs time to recover and heal. Sleep and mindfulness practices are just as essential as exercise and nutrition.

Winter Nutrition: Antioxidant-rich recipes for growth

Recipe: Warm winter glow bowl

Ingredients –

1 cup cooked Quinoa or Brown Rice
1 cup roasted sweet potato
1 cup steamed broccoli
½ cup pomegranate seeds
¼ cup toasted walnuts
Handful of baby spinach or kale
2 TBSP Tahini
1 TBSP Lemon Juice
1 TSP maple syrup
Salt & pepper to taste

Instructions:

- Layer the quinoa or brown rice in the bowl.
- Add the roasted sweet potatoes, broccoli, spinach, pomegranate seeds, and walnuts.

- In a different bowl whisk) together tahini, maple syrup, lemon juice, salt and pepper for the dressing.
- Drizzle the prepared dressing over the bowl and serve warm.

Benefits – Rich in antioxidants, fibre & omega 3. This bowl supports immunity, energy, and overall well-being.

Recipe: Spiced Orange & Ginger Tea

Ingredients –

4 cups water
2 oranges (zest & juice)
1 inch fresh ginger piece
2 cinnamon sticks
3 cloves
1 TBSP honey (optional)

Instructions:

- In a pot, combine water orange zest, ginger, cinnamon and cloves.
- Bring to a boil, then simmer for 10 minutes.
- Strain into cups & stir in orange juice & honey if required.

Benefits – Loaded with Vitamin C & Anti-inflammatory properties, this tea is the perfect winter tonic to fight oxidative stress.

Recipe: Spinach Soup

Ingredients –

2 cups fresh spinach leaves
1 small onion & tomato
2 cloves garlic
½ TSP black pepper
Salt as per taste
¼ TSP nutmeg

Instructions:

- Heat olive oil in a pan and saute onion, garlic, and tomato.
- Add spinach leaves and cook until wilted.

- Pour in the stock, bring it to a boil, and let it simmer and then turn off the flame.
- Allow the mixture to cool slightly, then blend until smooth using the blender.
- Pour back the soup to the pot, add nutmeg, black pepper, salt, and cook gently.
- Serve the soup in a bowl and enjoy warm.

Benefits – Rich in Iron, Vitamin C, and Antioxidants, provides hydration, warmth, and digestion. It keeps your skin glowing from within.

Recipe: Golden Glow Smoothie

Ingredients –

½ cup almond milk
1 cup orange juice
½ banana
¼ avocado
1 TSP turmeric powder
1 TSP cinnamon powder
1 TBSP chia seeds
1 TSP honey or maple syrup
A pinch of black pepper

Instructions:

- Add all the ingredients to a blender and blend until smooth and creamy.
- Pour the smoothie into a cup or bowl and garnish with sprinkles of cinnamon or pomegranate seeds.

Benefits – Nourishes from within by providing hydration, vitamins, & antioxidants.

Recipe: Ragi Almond Warm Porridge

Ingredients –

¼ cup ragi flour
2 cups milk
1 TBSP almond powder

1 TSP ghee
1 TSP jaggery powder or honey
A pinch of nutmeg
Chopped nuts & seeds (almonds, walnuts, pumpkin seeds)
Instructions –

- Heat ghee in a pan & light toast the ragi flour on low heat for 3 minutes until aromatic.
- Gradually add milk to the toasted ragi flour; stir continuously to avoid lumps.
- Let it cook on medium heat for 10 minutes, and stir occasionally until the mixture thickens.
- Now add jaggery, almond powder, cardamom powder, nutmeg, and mix well.
- Cook for another minute and turn off the flame.
- Pour the porridge into a bowl and top it with nuts and seeds for crunch and nutrition.

Benefits – it is not only warming & satisfying but also helps improve skin elasticity, strengthen immunity, and keep you energetic during the winter.

Manifesting Growth Beyond January

Manifestation requires consistency. Reflect weekly on your progress and celebrate each small win. Sitting with your thoughts will help you to stay connected with your vision.

Remember, growth is a journey, not a destination. Loving yourself with your flaws is the most potent tool you have for creating a vibrant and joyful future. With intent and nourishment, this January can start as a transformational year.

Here's to Manifesting Your Healthier and Happier Life

“"My well-being is a priority, and I am committed to nurturing it"”

Nourishing Hope: Transforming your health journey one step at a time

1. **The influence of surroundings and opinions**
   How societal & personal opinions can shape one's perception of health.
   Acknowledge the emotional challenges of navigating health amidst judgement or advice.
2. **Understanding past failure**
   Emphasize that setbacks are a part of growth, not an endpoint.
   Explore common reasons for past challenges, such as unrealistic goals or external pressures.
   Offer a reframing of failures as lessons for building resilience.
3. **The light of hope**
   Highlighting the power of intention and the role of hope in starting fresh.
   Share a relatable story about someone finding success by focusing on hope and persistence.
4. **The Baby-Step Approach**
   The importance of setting small, achievable goals rather than striving for perfection.
   For example:
   Incorporating one extra serving of vegetables
   swapping sugary drinks for water
   adding 5 minutes of walking to your routine
5. **Nutrition with Compassion**
   Encourage them to treat themselves with kindness and patience.
   Discuss the benefits of celebrating small victories to build momentum.

Conclusion: A new narrative for health

Let's rethink health together—not as something we "arrive at" but as an ongoing journey we're all on. Encourage the people around you to celebrate the little steps they take, no matter how small they seem. Every choice, every effort, adds up to something bigger—a life full of energy and well-being. Let's create a space where we support one another, where it's okay to grow at your own pace, and where we truly believe in our ability to make lasting, meaningful changes. Every small action matters—it's all part of the bigger picture of a healthier, happier life.

About the Writer

Swati Bhutani

With over seven years of experience, Swati Bhutani is a certified dietician known for her expertise in therapeutic diets and weight management. She blends clinical nutrition with Ayurvedic principles to create personalized wellness plans that address individual health needs. Holding a Postgraduate Diploma in Dietetics and Public Health Nutrition from Lady Irwin College and a Fellowship in Clinical Nutrition from Apollo Hospitals, she is skilled in managing conditions like diabetes, cardiovascular health, and hormonal balance. Through a compassionate, sustainable approach, she empowers clients to achieve lasting well-being.

VIII

Tarot Predictions for All Sun Signs in 2025: Career, Love, and Health

TAROT PREDICTIONS
FOR 2025

The year 2025 brings profound transformations, growth, and balance as the tarot cards reveal unique energies for each zodiac sign. This detailed prediction covers **Career & Finances**, **Love & Relationships**, and **Health** for all twelve sun signs. With clarity and insight, let's explore what 2025 holds for you.

Aries (March 21 - April 19): The High Priestess

The High Priestess represents intuition, inner wisdom, and patience. This year encourages Aries to trust their gut feelings and take time to reflect before making decisions. The decisions that come from the heart and intuition are likely to be more fruitful.

Career & Finances:

2025 will require you to balance your ambitions with patience. Instead of rushing into new projects, trust your instincts and gather all necessary information before acting. Financially, this is a good year to invest in education, skills, or personal growth. Be cautious with impulsive financial decisions.

Love & Relationships

The High Priestess asks you to deepen your emotional connections. For singles, a meaningful relationship may emerge, but patience is key. If you're already committed, prioritize open communication and understanding your partner's unspoken needs.

Health

Mental and emotional well-being take centre stage. Practicing meditation, journaling, or yoga will help you connect with your inner self. Avoid overworking and listen to your body's signals to maintain balance. Alternative healing and occult sciences will grab your attention and help you many ways this year.

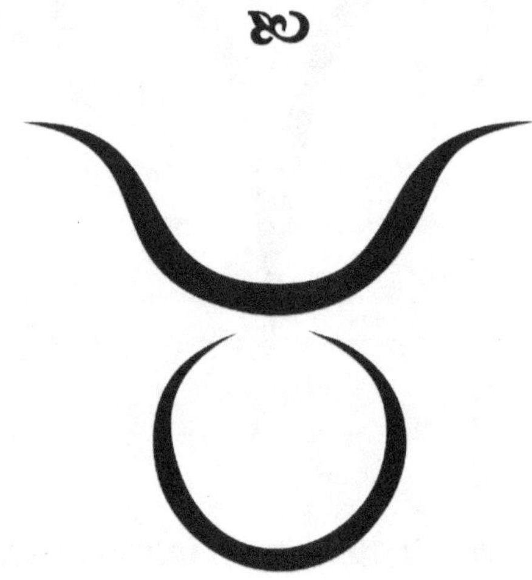

Taurus (April 20 - May 20): Six of Cups

The Six of Cups signifies nostalgia, harmony, and reconnecting with your roots. It encourages Taureans to find joy in simple moments and rekindle meaningful relationships this year.

Career & Finances

In 2025, your past efforts will bring positive results. A previous job opportunity or business idea may resurface, offering growth. Collaboration with familiar faces or trusted colleagues will prove fruitful. Financially, focus on saving and budgeting to ensure stability.

Love & Relationships

Love takes a warm, comforting tone this year. Singles may reconnect with someone from the past, while couples will experience renewed intimacy and joy. Cherishing shared memories will strengthen bonds. Perhaps visiting places that hold fond memories for you will help you reconnect with a renewed passion.

Health

Emotional healing is vital in 2025. Address lingering issues from the past and let go of grudges. Prioritize self-care routines and spend more time in nature to restore inner peace. Inner child healing work will help you deal with issues that stem from the past.

ꕤ

Gemini (May 21 - June 20): Death

The Death card symbolizes transformation, endings, and new beginnings. 2025 will be a year of letting go and embracing change for personal growth.

Career & Finances

A significant shift in your career may occur—whether it's changing jobs, roles, or directions. While this may feel overwhelming initially, these changes will lead you to better opportunities. Financially, reassess your budget and let go of habits or investments that no longer serve you.

Love & Relationships

Relationships will undergo transformation. Toxic or stagnant connections may end, making room for healthier bonds. Singles will find love by embracing their authentic selves. Existing relationships will deepen if both partners are willing to grow together.

Health

2025 calls for a reset in health habits. Focus on detoxification—both physically and emotionally. Let go of stress, unhealthy habits, and negative patterns to rejuvenate yourself fully.

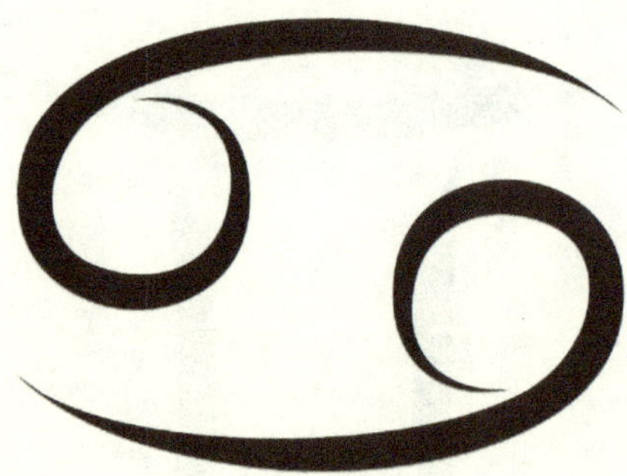

Cancer (June 21 - July 22): Ten of Wands

The Ten of Wands signifies burdens, responsibilities, and hard work. This year teaches you to manage your workload and seek balance.

Career & Finances

In 2025, hard work will dominate your career. You may feel overwhelmed by responsibilities, but perseverance will lead to success. Delegate tasks when necessary to avoid burnout. Financially, avoid overcommitting and set clear priorities.

Love & Relationships

Your personal relationships may require effort this year. Balancing work and love will be key. Singles might feel too burdened to pursue romance, but small efforts will pay off. For couples, supporting each other's goals will strengthen bonds.

Health

Stress management is crucial in 2025. Overworking can take a toll on your health. Regular exercise, sleep, and mindfulness practices will help you stay healthy and energetic.

ꙮ

Leo (July 23 - August 22): Eight of Pentacles

The Eight of Pentacles represents dedication, skill-building, and hard work. The focus for Leos this year will be on mastering their craft and achieving their goals.

Career & Finances

2025 is a productive year for Leo. Your dedication and efforts will bring success in your career. Whether you're starting a new project or improving current skills, consistency will pay off. Financially, smart planning and disciplined saving will lead to growth.

Love & Relationships

Leos in relationships will learn to balance love and work. Make time for your partner despite your busy schedule. Singles may find love through work-related connections or shared passions.

Health

This year requires you to focus on a disciplined health routine. Regular workouts and mindful eating will help you maintain energy and stamina for your goals.

Virgo (August 23 - September 22): Three of Pentacles

The Three of Pentacles signifies teamwork, collaboration, and skill-building. 2025 encourages Virgos to work with others to achieve success.

Career & Finances

Your career will flourish through collaboration and learning from others. Teamwork and building strong relationships at work will bring recognition and growth. Financially, shared ventures or investments will bring positive results.

Love & Relationships

Open communication and cooperation are vital for relationships. Couples will work together to build a stable foundation, while singles may meet someone through group activities or mutual friends.

Health

Focus on improving your lifestyle by incorporating routines that support long-term well-being. Regular exercise, healthy meals, and a balanced mindset will keep you thriving.

Libra (September 23 - October 22): King of Pentacles

The King of Pentacles represents stability, success, and abundance. Libras will enjoy material and emotional growth in 2025.

Career & Finances

This year brings financial success and professional stability. Promotions, investments, or new opportunities will strengthen your career. Manage your wealth wisely and consider long-term financial plans.

Love & Relationships

Relationships will feel stable and secure. Couples will experience loyalty and harmony, while singles may attract a dependable and grounded partner.

Health

Prioritize physical health by adopting a consistent wellness routine. Strength-building exercises and nutritious food will help you feel strong and grounded. Avoid overindulging in anything, especially food.

Scorpio (October 23 - November 21): Ten of Swords

The Ten of Swords represents endings, release, and new beginnings. Scorpio will face challenges but emerge stronger.

Career & Finances

2025 marks the end of difficult phases in your career. While setbacks may occur, they will clear the path for new opportunities. Financially, avoid unnecessary risks and focus on rebuilding stability.

Love & Relationships

Relationships may face challenges that demand closure or healing. Letting go of toxic connections will free you for healthier relationships. Singles will find love after releasing emotional baggage.

Health

Prioritize recovery and healing. Address mental and physical exhaustion through rest, therapy, and supportive practices.

Sagittarius (November 22 - December 21): Three of Cups

The Three of Cups signifies celebration, friendship, and joy. 2025 will be a year of happiness and meaningful connections.

Career & Finances

Collaborative projects and teamwork will bring success. Celebrating small milestones at work will keep you motivated. Financially, shared investments or group ventures will prove beneficial.

Love & Relationships

This is a joyful year for love and friendships. Singles may find romance through social gatherings, while couples will celebrate milestones and deepen their connection. Family get-togethers are on the cards.

Health

Focus on emotional well-being and fun activities. Surrounding yourself with supportive people will keep you energized and happy.

Capricorn (December 22 - January 19): Eight of Wands

The Eight of Wands represents movement, speed, and progress. Capricorns will experience rapid growth and changes in 2025.

Career & Finances

Expect sudden opportunities or advancements in your career. Your hard work will bring quick results. Financially, positive changes like new income streams or investments will occur.

Love & Relationships

Love will move swiftly this year. Singles may experience whirlwind romances, while couples will strengthen their bond through shared adventures and experiences.

Health

Maintain energy by staying active and adopting a fast-paced but balanced lifestyle. Prioritize rest between busy periods.

Aquarius (January 20 - February 18): Ace of Pentacles

The Ace of Pentacles represents new beginnings, abundance, and opportunities. Aquarius will see growth in many areas of life.

Career & Finances

New career opportunities or financial prospects will emerge. This is an excellent year for starting new ventures, investments, or learning skills that increase income.

Love & Relationships

Relationships will feel fresh and exciting. Singles will attract grounded and stable partners, while couples will build stronger emotional and financial foundations.

Health

Focus on improving physical health with mindful eating and regular exercise. Fresh starts in lifestyle habits will boost vitality.

Pisces (February 19 - March 20): Page of Swords

The Page of Swords represents curiosity, communication, and learning. Pisces will focus on expanding knowledge and improving clarity in 2025.

Career & Finances

Be open to new learning opportunities in your career. Networking and clear communication will help you grow professionally. Financially, focus on gathering knowledge before making big decisions.

Love & Relationships

Relationships will require open and honest communication. Singles may attract someone intellectual, while couples will strengthen bonds through meaningful conversations.

Health

Prioritize mental clarity and avoid overthinking. Activities like reading, puzzles, or mindfulness will keep your mind sharp and stress-free.

Final Thoughts

The tarot cards for 2025 offer guidance, hope, and direction for all sun signs. By embracing the lessons of each card, you can navigate challenges and make the most of opportunities throughout the year. Trust the journey, stay balanced, and focus on personal growth for a fulfilling 2025.

About the Writer

Meetu Sehgal

Meetu Sehgal is a Personal Transformation and Emotional Wellness Coach, EFT Trainer, Tarot Reader, Author, Reiki Grandmaster and Counselling Psychologist. With more than 15 years of experience in her field, she has been passionately working with individuals, helping them resolve health, wealth and relationship challenges through coaching. Meetu Sehgal is an MBA graduate from Delhi University and also holds a Masters in Psychology. Passionate about writing and spirituality, she has blended both in her work, which has helped hundreds of people around the world find peace within themselves. Her latest book, "Happy Inside Out", is a definitive guide to understanding and handling emotions and moods.

Spirit Speak

Wisdom through the ages

IX
Ancient Wisdom for Modern Living

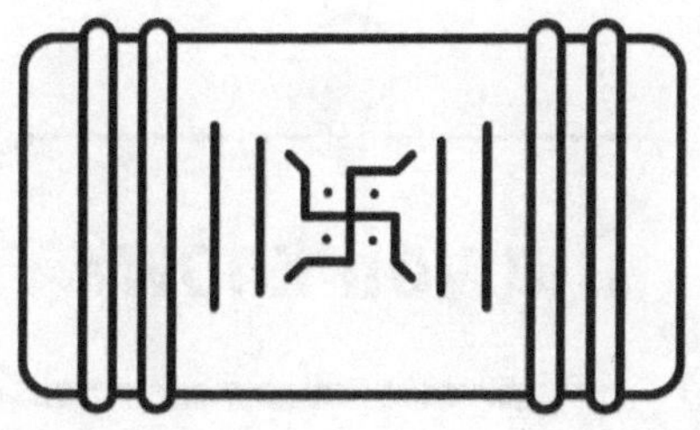

“*"Mana eva manushyanam karanam bandha mokshayoho."*
(The mind alone is the cause of bondage and liberation.)
-Manusmriti”

Meaning: Your thoughts shape your reality. A restless mind leads to suffering, while a disciplined mind opens the path to freedom and happiness. Cultivate mindfulness to unlock your highest potential.

X

Meaning behind the Rituals: Surya Arghya

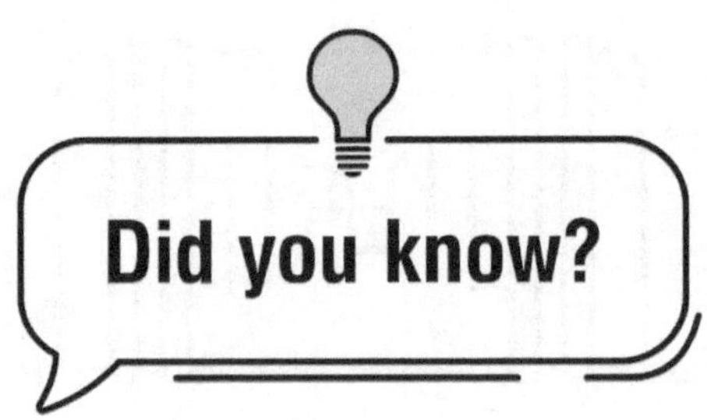

The ritual of offering water to the Sun, known as "**Surya Arghya**" is deeply rooted in Vedic traditions. Though it is primarily considered a spiritual act, it also has scientific and practical significance. Here's a breakdown of the scientific meaning:

- The exposure to sunlight during this time helps regulate the body's **circadian rhythm** (biological clock), which governs sleep, hormonal balance, and overall energy levels.
- Morning sunlight triggers the production of serotonin, a hormone that enhances mood and well-being.

- Standing in the early sunlight with minimal exposure (like while offering water) enhances Vitamin D synthesis without the harmful effects of intense midday sun.
- Viewing sunlight through this refracted spectrum can reduce the intensity of direct sunlight on the eyes, providing a soothing visual effect and preventing strain.
- The act of sprinkling or pouring water also has a psychological cooling effect, which is calming to the mind.
- The act of pouring water on the ground increases the level of negative ions in the surrounding air, especially when done on soil or natural surfaces. Negative ions are known to purify the air, reduce stress, and enhance mood.
- While offering water, individuals often stand barefoot on the ground, hold their posture upright, and focus on the act, which aids in **grounding** and increases the flow of **prana** (life energy).
- Morning sunlight contains **infrared rays** that improve blood circulation, relax muscles, and promote healing.
- Rituals provide a structured start to the day, reinforcing discipline and mindfulness.

The ritual of offering water to the Sun is a blend of spiritual reverence and scientific wisdom. It harmonizes the body's biological processes with natural cycles, enhancing physical, mental, and emotional health while fostering a deeper connection to nature.

XI
Affirmation for the Month

"The universe is always working in my favour, always."

About Ezine Kaleidoscope

In this new age, the definition and meaning of the word 'Spirituality' has become varied and is often misconstrued with fear, religion and a monk sitting in meditation on a lonely Himalayan mountain.

But spirituality is much beyond this faulty image. It is an inherent part of who we are. Because truly, we are spiritual beings having a human experience.

The purpose of Ezine Kaleidoscope is to bring the true essence of spirituality to our readers and make it so accessible that it doesn't feel like an alien overwhelming concept anymore. Our aim is to make it a part of everyone's everyday life.

"*If every living moment can be full of awareness, there will be joy and bliss in the world*
-Meetu Sehgal
"

Ezine Kaleidoscope's journey began in November 2010 as a journey towards spirituality, awareness and making the spiritual tools accessible to all in a simple understandable manner.

It is our vision and mission to create awareness and remove the element of fear from spirituality and all things related. It is vested in light and that's what we want to bring to the life of everyone who reads us.

Know more about us

Website: ezinekaleidoscope.com
Email: info@ezinekaleidoscope.com
Instagram: @Ezine.Kaleidoscope
Facebook: www.facebook.com/ezineKaleidoscope

SUBSCRIPTION DETAILS

Unlock a world of spiritual wisdom and personal growth with Kaleidoscope Ezine. Each issue brings you insightful articles on mindfulness, healing, and self-discovery. Join our community of readers committed to living balanced, fulfilling lives.

YEARLY SUBSCRIPTION

INR 1800

Yearly Subscription ₹1800 (for 12 issues)
You Save 25%! Enjoy each issue for just ₹150 instead of ₹200.

With a yearly subscription, you'll get:

1. Exclusive access to all 12 print or digital issues of Ezine Kaleidoscope.
2. Early access to special editions and bonus content.

PRICE PER ISSUE

₹200

3. Special invitations to subscriber-only events and workshops.
4. 10% discount for all the workshops and events for the period of subscription.

Don't miss out on a full year of spiritual wisdom and insights at a great value!

Scan The QR Code For Subscription

www.ingramcontent.com/pod-product-compliance
Lightning Source LLC
LaVergne TN
LVHW040951150826
845672LV00002B/646

* 9 7 9 8 8 9 6 7 3 2 9 7 6 *